Building
Grammar

Grades 7-8

by
Rhonda Chapman

Published by Instructional Fair
an imprint of
Frank Schaffer Publications®

Instructional Fair

Author: Rhonda Chapman
Editors: Sara Bierling, Meredith Van Zomeren, Wendy Roh Jenks, Jane Haradine
Illustrations: Dave Winter

Frank Schaffer Publications®

Instructional Fair is an imprint of Frank Schaffer Publications.

Send all inquiries to:
Frank Schaffer Publications
3195 Wilson Drive NW
Grand Rapids, Michigan 49534

Building Grammar—grades 7-8

ISBN: 0-7424-0152-9

6 7 8 9 10 11 12 PAT 10 09 08 07

Table of Contents

Hanukkah

> **noun**—person, place, or thing
> **adjective**—modifies a noun
> **preposition**—relates a noun or pronoun to another word or clause
> **conjunction**—links two or more words or groups of words
> **verb**—shows an action or a state of being
> **adverb**—modifies a verb
> **article**—a, an, the (modifies nouns)
> **pronoun**—can be singular, plural, or possessive; takes the place of a noun
> **interjection**—a word or phrase used in exclamation to express emotion

Read the narrative below and determine the part of speech of the word that follows each number. Write the part of speech from the box above on the corresponding line below.

My family observes Hanukkah, an (1.) important holiday celebrated by Jewish people. (2.) It begins each year on the twenty-fifth day of the Hebrew month of Kislev (3.) and lasts eight days. (4.) Hanukkah usually falls (5.) in December.

Hanukkah is (6.) a time of gift giving and game playing, too. The children (7.) receive gifts and sing songs. (8.) Wow, can you believe we children sometimes get money during Hanukkah? One of my favorite things to do is play with the dreidel, which is used to play games during the (9.) holiday. The dreidel is a (10.) toplike toy with a Hebrew letter (11.) inscribed on each side.

During Hanukkah, we (12.) joyously celebrate the history of our people and our religion.

1. _____
2. _____
3. _____
4. _____
5. _____
6. _____
7. _____
8. _____
9. _____
10. _____
11. _____
12. _____

Crispy Critters

A **conjunction** is a word that is used to join words or groups of words.

> Dogs **and** wolves howl.
> I am happy, **for** today I bought a kitten.

Conjunction Bank

neither	nor	either	or	and	not only
but also	while	so	for	yet	

Write a conjunction in each of the blanks below to complete the Crispy Critters advertisement. Use each conjunction once, but use **and** three times.

Some cats are treated like pets, _____ others are treated like family. Show your favorite feline that you love _____ respect him by bringing home CRISPY CRITTERS kitty food! CRISPY CRITTERS will _____ make your cat happier _____ more energetic and lively. CRISPY CRITTERS comes in four tasty flavors, _____ choose his favorite. Select _____ chicken, beef, _____ seafood. Other cat foods claim to satisfy most cats, _____ don't back their claims with research. You can be sure that when you buy CRISPY CRITTERS you will _____ waste money _____ disappoint your feline friends. CRISPY CRITTERS is delicious _____ nutritious _____ a hit every time. Buy CRISPY CRITTERS today, _____ every day your cat will thank you!

Let's Get Together

Contractions tie two words together to make a new word. An apostrophe takes the place of the letter that has been removed.

let + us = let's
that + would = that'd

Write the two small words in each equation that have been put together to make each contraction.

1. can't   = _____ + _____   9. won't   = _____ + _____
2. aren't   = _____ + _____   10. hadn't   = _____ + _____
3. don't   = _____ + _____   11. shouldn't = _____ + _____
4. doesn't = _____ + _____   12. needn't = _____ + _____
5. isn't   = _____ + _____   13. couldn't = _____ + _____
6. hasn't   = _____ + _____   14. weren't = _____ + _____
7. mustn't = _____ + _____   15. didn't   = _____ + _____
8. haven't = _____ + _____   16. mightn't = _____ + _____

Combine each set of words below to make more contractions.

1. I am   _____   5. could have   _____
2. he will   _____   6. I had   _____
3. it is   _____   7. we are   _____
4. they had _____   8. we will   _____

At the Front

A **prefix** is one or more syllables added to the beginning of a word to form a new word.

un + believer = unbeliever
mis + trust = mistrust
off + shoot = offshoot

Match a prefix with a root word to form a new word.

_____	1. anti	A.	merge
_____	2. tele	B.	claim
_____	3. sub	C.	call
_____	4. under	D.	live
_____	5. pro	E.	ordinary
_____	6. en	F.	cover
_____	7. re	G.	freeze
_____	8. out	H.	courage
_____	9. extra	I.	meter
_____	10. peri	J.	phone

_____	1. post	A.	eager
_____	2. bi	B.	tanker
_____	3. co	C.	organized
_____	4. mini	D.	clockwise
_____	5. over	E.	cycle
_____	6. extra	F.	fine
_____	7. super	G.	violent
_____	8. non	H.	author
_____	9. ultra	I.	skirt
_____	10. counter	J.	war

Bring up the Rear

A **suffix** is one or more syllables added to the end of a word to form a new word. A letter is usually dropped from the original word.

love + able = lovable   *motion + less = motionless*

Complete the classified ads by adding suffixes to the words that are followed by a blank line.

-ing   -dom   -able   -ment   -ship   -ade   -ure   -ful   -ness   -ance

---

The School Times   **Classified**   May 2000

Help Wanted

ARE YOU SUFFER_____ from bore_____? You can have a pleasur(e)_____ summer work_____ at the **Thunder Caverns Amuse_____ Park**. For information, call 1-800-FUN-SOAK.

Meetings

Your attend_____ is welcome at the town meet_____. We will discuss issues of free_____ and citi-zen_____.

Demand fair_____ and good treat_____ for your pigs. They are pets, too! Come and speak about your concerns for our lov(e)_____ swine.

For Sale

FRESH AND DELICIOUS lemon_____ and butter cookies with lemon ic(e)_____ made by the varsity cheerleaders.

South City's soccer team is sell_____ chocolate bars. Buy several and enjoy the sweet_____!

Tutoring

DOES ALGEBRA HAVE YOU feel_____ like a fail_____? Sign up for tutor_____. It's help____ and fun. Call Mr. X for info.

FINISH HIGH SCHOOL and begin your adult life with wis(e)_____! A diploma puts you on the path to a success_____ life.

The Short of It

> Use **abbreviations** with other words or names; never use them by themselves. Avoid using abbreviations in text. You should spell out abbreviated words when they appear in a sentence. Capitalize the abbreviations of proper nouns.
>
> *I live at 1315 Trail <u>ct.</u>, Madison, <u>oh</u> 21461.* (incorrect)
> *My address: 1315 Trail <u>Ct.</u>, Madison, <u>OH</u> 21461* (correct)
>
> *Christmas is in <u>Dec.</u>* (incorrect)
> <u>*Dec.*</u> *25, 2002* (correct)

Match each word with its abbreviation.

_____ 1. apartment	_____ 7. Incorporated	A. Rd.	G. pp.
_____ 2. volume	_____ 8. Company	B. cont.	H. vol.
_____ 3. Road	_____ 9. continued	C. Inc.	I. misc.
_____ 4. Reverend	_____ 10. Corporation	D. Corp.	J. lat.
_____ 5. miscellaneous	_____ 11. anonymous	E. Rev.	K. Co.
_____ 6. latitude	_____ 12. pages	F. apt.	L. anon.

In the blanks, write **C** if the abbreviation is used correctly; write **N** if it is not.

_____ 1. We live in an apt.

_____ 2. Apt. 303, Sudsby Rd.

_____ 3. Rev. Martin

_____ 4. My father works for a big corp.

_____ 5. For homework, we were assigned pp. 94–115 in *Great Expectations.*

_____ 6. I hate to watch a show that will be cont. the next day.

_____ 7. Please turn down the vol.

_____ 8. We used money from the misc. category of our budget to buy the gift.

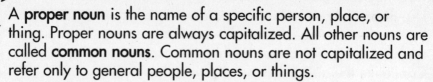

Louisa May Alcott

common and proper nouns

> A **proper noun** is the name of a specific person, place, or thing. Proper nouns are always capitalized. All other nouns are called **common nouns**. Common nouns are not capitalized and refer only to general people, places, or things.
>
> **proper nouns**: *Joseph, England, Vermont, Pepsi*
> **common nouns**: *boy, country, state, beverage*

Underline all the common nouns. Circle the proper nouns.

1. Louisa May Alcott is remembered as a great American author.

2. She was born in Germantown, Pennsylvania, on November 29, 1832.

3. She considered Ralph Waldo Emerson and Henry David Thoreau her friends.

4. Louisa grew up in a poor family in New England where she made and sold dolls' clothes to earn money.

5. When she was a little older, she taught school and began writing.

6. In 1854, Miss Alcott published her first book, titled *Flower Fables*.

7. Several of her stories were published in *Atlantic Monthly*.

8. Eventually, she wrote *Little Women,* a semi-autobiographical novel.

9. Other books based on Alcott's life include *Little Men* and *Jo's Boys*.

10. Today, readers can enjoy her biography *Invincible Louisa,* written by Cornelia Meigs.

Patches on Jackets

> **Plural nouns** represent more than one.

According to the rule given, write the plural form of each of the following words.

To form the plural of most nouns, just add **s**. If the noun ends in *s, x, ch, sh, z,* or *ss*, add **es**.

1. (jacket) _____   4. (dress) _____
2. (shirt) _____   5. (sash) _____
3. (sock) _____   6. (swatch) _____

For nouns that end in *y* preceded by a vowel, just add **s**. For nouns that end in *y* preceded by a consonant, change the *y* to *i* and add **es**.

1. (boy) _____   4. (treaty) _____
2. (tray) _____   5. (ploy) _____
3. (spray) _____   6. (mystery) _____

To form the plural of a word that ends in an *o* preceded by a vowel, add **s**. For words that end in an *o* preceded by a consonant, usually add **es**. (There are some exceptions to this rule.)

1. (tomato) _____   4. (zoo) _____
2. (avocado) _____   5. (hero) _____
3. (buffalo) _____   6. (stereo) _____

For words that end in *f* or *fe*, change the *f* to *v* and add **es**; some of these words simply add **s**. (You may need to consult a dictionary to be certain.)

1. (scarf) _____   4. (chief) _____
2. (knife) _____   5. (shelf) _____
3. (leaf) _____   6. (elf) _____

Concrete or Asphalt?

abstract and concrete nouns

An **abstract noun** names an idea, quality, or state of mind.
A **concrete noun** names something that can be seen or touched.

abstract nouns: peace, patience, success, sadness
concrete nouns: road, flower, house, animal, Joe

Circle the concrete nouns. Underline the abstract nouns.

Tony	cement	ambition	idea	land
trust	muscle	precipitation	grace	hope
excitement	talent	sidewalk	honor	faith
New York	sweetness	gravel	influence	hardhat
road	shovel	truck	zero	skyscraper
bucket	power	water	terror	beauty
building	argument	legacy	rock	disgrace
mixer	victory	preference	trowel	love
street	fidelity	asphalt	money	commitment
pride	wood	glue	hate	air
fear	integrity	dog	book	man
music	evil	cooperation	sweat	improvement

Marching Pride

Nouns that show ownership are called **possessive nouns**. To form the possessive of a singular noun add **'s**. If a noun is already in the plural form and ends in an *s*, simply add an apostrophe. If the plural form does not end in an *s*, add **'s**.

singular possessive nouns: *Cindy's chair, dog's bone, piano's keys*
plural possessive nouns: *ladies' purses, houses' windows, children's lunches, women's club*

Rewrite the phrases by using possessive nouns.

1. Drumsticks belonging to drummers

   _____

2. The reed of the clarinet

   _____

3. Baton belonging to the drum major

   _____

4. Instruments of the musicians

   _____

5. Sound of the tubas

   _____

6. Colorful flags of the color guard

   _____

7. Slide belonging to the trombone

   _____

8. Crash made by cymbals

   _____

9. New uniforms owned by the band

   _____

All Together!

A **collective noun** names a group of people, places, or things. When a collective noun refers to a group as a unit, it is considered singular. When it refers to the individual members of the group who are acting separately, it is considered plural.

singular collective nouns:
The **school** of fish live in the cool water.
Our **team** usually wins.

plural collective nouns:
The **school** of fish are all swimming in different directions to avoid the predator.
The **team** are all expected to earn good grades in school.

Match the collective nouns.

_____	1. colony	A.	cotton
_____	2. fleet	B.	ships
_____	3. squad	C.	lies
_____	4. grove	D.	geese
_____	5. bale	E.	diamonds
_____	6. gaggle	F.	ants
_____	7. pack	G.	police
_____	8. nest	H.	cards
_____	9. cluster	I.	snakes
_____	10. deck	J.	trees

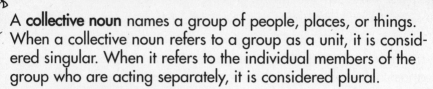

Mark the following collective nouns **S** (singular) or **P** (plural). Circle the correct verb.

_____ 1. The family (is, are) all opening their gifts together.

_____ 2. Grandma's batch of cookies (is, are) baking in the oven.

_____ 3. Mom's set of Christmas china (is, are) waiting on the table.

_____ 4. The cleaning staff (is, are) not working today; they are home with their families.

_____ 5. The company (is, are) due to arrive soon.

Cold-Blooded

predicate nouns

> A **predicate noun** is a noun used as a subject complement (the subject of the sentence and the predicate noun represent the same thing). Predicate nouns follow linking verbs.
>
> *Leo was the fiercest lion in the zoo.*
> *Leo = lion*

In each of the following sentences, circle the simple subject and underline the simple predicate noun. Then complete the equation.

1. Reptiles are a specific group of animals.

   _____ = _____

2. They are creatures that are cold-blooded.

   _____ = _____

3. A snake is a reptile.

   _____ = _____

4. The swamp is home to many snakes.

   _____ = _____

5. Iguanas are also members of the reptile family.

   _____ = _____

6. They are lizards that have spines from head to toe.

   _____ = _____

7. The desert is a good habitat for a variety of snakes and lizards.

   _____ = _____

8. The huge dinosaurs that once roamed the earth were reptiles.

   _____ = _____

9. Tyrannosaurus was a flesh-eating dinosaur that lived on land.

   _____ = _____

Published by Instructional Fair. Copyright protected.   15   0-7424-0152-9 *Building Grammar*

Colorful Clues

When a pronoun is the subject of the sentence, it is called a **subject pronoun**. When a pronoun is used as the direct object, indirect object, or object of the preposition, it is called an **object pronoun**. A pronoun must agree with its antecedent in both number and gender.

She dropped the book. (subject)
Eric picked *it* up. (direct object)
Betsy gave *him* a big smile. (indirect object)
Eric would do anything for *her*. (object of the preposition)

Underline the pronoun in each sentence. On the line, write **S** if the pronoun is a subject; write **O** if the pronoun is an object.

_____ 1. Elephants wear it.

_____ 2. It is as dark as the darkest night.

_____ 3. Grandma gave us slippers that perfectly match the delicate hue on the inside of a rabbit's ear.

_____ 4. I bought a chocolate-colored sweater when I was shopping at the mall.

_____ 5. He has eyes that sparkle like beautiful ocean water.

_____ 6. I am the acronym for all the colors of the rainbow.

_____ 7. The shirt that looks like electric sunshine belongs to him.

_____ 8. Kathryn described to her the cat's fur, which was like fluffy clouds on a sunny day.

_____ 9. We are thinking about painting the exterior of the house the color of pumpkin.

_____ 10. Larry told me that Joe prefers the color of money.

_____ 11. Grapes that had been dipped in nature's royal paint appeared all around him.

_____ 12. Apples, cherries, and some fast cars are dressed in it.

Shoes Galore

An **antecedent** is the noun to which a pronoun refers. The antecedent may be in the same sentence as the pronoun, or it may appear in another sentence nearby.

*The **guys** shined their shoes after **they** finished walking through the mud.* (*they* refers to *guys*)

Read the paragraph below. Draw an arrow from each italicized pronoun to its antecedent.

My family has a large shoe closet in *our* vestibule. *It* is a mess because everyone just kicks *their* shoes inside. If you would dig through that pile you would find many different kinds of footwear in *it*; my brother's cleats, Mom's three-inch high heels, and Dad's dirty work boots are among *them*. My sister Maggie has about a hundred pairs of shoes. *She* has red cowboy boots, summer sandals, weird-looking clogs, and running shoes, just to name a few. *They* are all in the heap. The pile is growing bigger, and *it* is a pain in the neck. Finding a matching pair in that mess takes forever. Someone needs to clean *it* up. I think I'll tell my sister that *she* has to do it!

Sports Fanatics

> An **indefinite pronoun** is one that refers generally, not specifically, to people, places, or things. Some indefinite pronouns are always singular, some are always plural, and some may be either singular or plural.
>
> *singular indefinite pronouns:* anyone, everyone, no one, someone, something
>
> *plural indefinite pronouns:* many, both, few, several, others
>
> *singular or plural indefinite pronouns:* all, any, most, some, none

In each of the following sentences, underline the indefinite pronouns. Circle the verb that agrees in number with the indefinite pronoun acting as the subject.

1. Everyone in my family (love, loves) to watch football on Sunday afternoons.

2. Several of my friends and I (play, plays) baseball.

3. After school, some of the guys (practice, practices) basketball on our street.

4. In our little town, no one (know, knows) much about ice hockey.

5. Many (choose, chooses) tennis, while others (prefer, prefers) racquetball.

6. All of the schools in our community (has, have) soccer teams.

7. Does anyone (consider, considers) pool a sport?

8. Someone in our class (claim, claims) table tennis is an Olympic sport.

9. In the ring, both boxers (take, takes) a beating.

10. Each speed skater (race, races) against the clock to get the best time possible.

11. Fortunately, somebody (was able, were able) to get us tickets to the ice-skating competition.

Peanuts

> A **possessive pronoun** is one that indicates ownership or possession. Possessive pronouns include: **my, mine, your, yours, his, her, hers, its, our, ours, their, theirs.**
>
> *He forgot **his** peanuts as he raced out of school.*

Read the story, underline all of the pronouns and circle all of the possessive pronouns.

Lou loved peanuts. Lou's mom bought huge amounts of peanuts to keep him satisfied. But, despite her attempts, her son's ravenous appetite for peanuts grew with each passing day. Lou carried them in his pockets, which bulged like satchels at his waist. Everywhere we went he shucked his peanuts, leaving a crunchy trail of shells behind him. The problem increased until our gym teacher finally refused to let him play volleyball after all the players began slipping on his shellings. Our teammates lost their patience, too, and suggested Lou sit out. He protested, but our team just yelled, "You're through, Lou!"

Then, on Saturday, Lou met his terrible fate. While enjoying a riveting performance at the circus and munching feverishly on his favorite snack, my friend Lou was attacked by a hungry baby elephant. She apparently broke free when she smelled Lou's pocketful of peanuts. She thought the peanuts should be hers. And so, Lou's peanut-eating days are at an end. It pains me to report the conclusion of this tale about a dear friend of mine. Poor Lou, we will miss you.

Published by Instructional Fair. Copyright protected.   19   0-7424-0152-9 *Building Grammar*

Pearls

Relative pronouns are used to introduce groups of words that modify nouns. **Interrogative pronouns** introduce questions.

relative pronouns: who, whose, which, that
People **who** read a lot are often very intelligent.

interrogative pronouns: who, whom, whose, what, which
Whose book is this?

Circle the relative pronouns in the paragraph.

The book that I read for my report really made me think. *The Pearl*, which was written by John Steinbeck, is a parable about survival and overcoming oppression. I am one who has faced little prejudice in my life, yet there are many other people who struggle their entire lives to break free of injustice. These men and women, whose lives exemplify the test of perseverance, inspire me. I appreciate the story that Steinbeck told, which demonstrates very well the power of oppression and the importance of perseverance.

Underline the relative and interrogative pronouns in each sentence below. Write an **I** if it is interrogative; write an **R** if it is relative.

_____ 1. Whose pearl necklace is this?

_____ 2. She wore pearls that were creamy white.

_____ 3. My mom, who is a pearl lover, owns many beautiful pieces of pearl jewelry.

_____ 4. A perfect pearl, which is formed in an oyster, can be extremely valuable.

_____ 5. Which color pearl do you prefer?

_____ 6. Hey, to whom does this pearl necklace belong?

_____ 7. I prefer black pearls, which are beautiful and unusual.

G-nip, G-nop

> **Reflexive pronouns** are formed by adding *self* or *selves* to certain forms of personal pronouns. They reflect the action of the verb back to the subject. **Intensive pronouns** are formed in the same way, but they give intensity back to the noun or pronoun just named.
>
> *reflexive*: I taught **myself** to play table tennis.
> *intensive*: The table **itself** comes from the sports shop down the street.

Underline the reflexive and intensive pronouns in the sentences below. Write an **R** if the pronoun is reflexive; write an **I** if it is intensive.

_____ 1. We all taught ourselves to play table tennis.

_____ 2. The table itself stands in our basement.

_____ 3. Dad himself carried it downstairs on Andrew's eleventh birthday.

_____ 4. I myself couldn't wait to grab a paddle and start playing.

_____ 5. The boys immediately placed themselves around the game table.

_____ 6. Christina proclaimed herself a pro.

_____ 7. You are probably asking yourself who actually played the first game.

_____ 8. It was Mom herself who made the first challenge.

_____ 9. My father himself quickly accepted it, and they began to play.

_____ 10. They played themselves into an intensely competitive sweat.

_____ 11. We took turns teaching ourselves to volley the ball back and forth.

_____ 12. I myself like the game so much that I can play for hours each day.

Case of the Missing Cow

> The use of **who** and **whom** is determined by the pronoun's function in the clause. Generally, **who** is used as the subject of a sentence or a clause. **Whom** is used as the object (direct, indirect, or object of the preposition).
>
> *Who* is a suspect?
> With *whom* did you see the cow last night?

Read the sentences below and circle the correct pronoun.

1. Farmer Frank is the one (who, whom) owns the cow.

2. Steve Grant is the officer in (who, whom) Farmer Frank has placed his trust to find her.

3. Do you know (who, whom) has taken Farmer Frank's cow Bessie?

4. Farmer Frank's wife, (who, whom) gave the cow as a gift, has been crying since Bessie's disappearance.

5. (Who, Whom) would want a huge plastic cow anyway?

6. The police at the station to (who, whom) she spoke have tried to calm her down.

7. There is a rumor that someone (who, whom) is planning a harmless prank has taken the plastic bovine.

8. To (who, whom) was this information given?

9. Mrs. McGrady is the one (who, whom) heard that the cow might show up on the high school roof.

10. She did not know (who, whom) might be instigating such a stunt.

11. The students (who, whom) attend Dairyville High are being questioned.

12. No one seems to know anything about those (who, whom) are involved.

13. Farmer Frank released a statement saying that he was not angry with the pranksters (who, whom) have borrowed his cow, but he is asking that they return her unharmed.

14. Officer Grant is the one with (who, whom) you should speak if you have any information about Bessie, the missing cow.

Dazzling Stars

A **verb** is a word that expresses an action or a state of being.
  action: *cry, leap, laugh, win, peel*
  state of being: *looks, is, are, were, seems*

Circle all of the verbs in the poster below. Then write the verbs under the appropriate category.

Action Verbs

1. _____
2. _____
3. _____
4. _____
5. _____
6. _____
7. _____
8. _____
9. _____
10. _____
11. _____
12. _____

State of Being Verbs

1. _____
2. _____
3. _____
4. _____
5. _____

Dazzling Stars
Traveling Circus
Presents

- Crazy, unicycle-riding clowns are experts who make children smile.

- Trapeze artists fly through the air performing awesome stunts.

- Curly poodles are dressed in frills and dance for everyone's enjoyment.

- The thousand-pound man is a sight to behold.

- Elegant horses seem royal as they prance and bow with pride.

- Daredevil Dave shoots himself out of a cannon with terrifying speed.

- Talented tumblers look beautiful in glittery costumes and amaze young and old alike.

- The knife thrower displays his skill and bravery as he flings sharpened blades.

Volcanoes

A **verb** must agree with its **subject** in number. A singular subject requires a singular verb, and a plural subject requires a plural verb. Note: The number of a subject is not changed by a phrase or a clause that might follow it.

singular: The volcano erupts. The volcano, which has looked threatening for hours, erupts.

plural: The volcanoes erupt. The volcanoes that line the mountaintop erupt.

In the following sentences, circle the correct verb.

1. Volcanic eruptions (occur, occurs) when magma (rise, rises) through the earth's crust and emerges onto the surface.

2. Magma that (erupt, erupts) onto the earth's surface (is, are) called lava.

3. Just about all types of lava (contain, contains) silicon and oxygen.

4. When lava flows over the earth, the land that lies in its path (is destroyed, are destroyed).

5. Most Hawaiian eruptions (is, are) gentle.

6. Some others (blast, blasts) huge amounts of volcanic ash high into the air.

7. After a powerful blast, volcanic ash (settle, settles) everywhere.

8. Volcanic islands (emerge, emerges) from the ocean when ash and lava (build, builds) up over years.

9. Legend (say, says) that when Pele, the volcano goddess, becomes angry, she causes volcanoes to erupt.

Chocolate

> The **tense** of a verb indicates the time in which an action takes place. **Present tense** indicates action or a state of being that is happening now. **Past tense** indicates action or a state of being that has been completed. **Future tense** indicates action or a state of being that will take place. The auxiliary verb *will* is usually used with the principal verb to form the future tense.
>
> I **eat** chocolate kisses.
> I **ate** chocolate kisses.
> I **will eat** chocolate kisses.

Underline the verb in each sentence. Identify the tense of each verb by marking **P** (present tense), **PA** (past tense), or **F** (future tense).

_____ 1. Delicious chocolate comes from bumpy green pods grown on tropical trees in Central and South America.

_____ 2. The Aztecs treasured chocolate beans nearly as much as we value gold.

_____ 3. The trees that produced these valuable beans were called *kakahuatl* (ca-ca-hoo-AH-tul) by the Aztecs.

_____ 4. Today the kakahuatl tree is called the cacao (cah-COW) tree.

_____ 5. Because it was so costly, only rich Aztecs drank chocolatl (show-co-LAH-tul).

_____ 6. Cacao trees are grown in tropical countries around the world.

_____ 7. Cacao trees have long, shiny bright green leaves with bunches of little flowers on their football-shaped pods.

_____ 8. If you break open a pod, you will find twenty to forty semi-purple cacao beans.

_____ 9. The cacao beans are bitter until they soak in their sweet pulp for several days.

_____ 10. Then they will be dried in the sun.

Origami Bird

An **infinitive** is a present tense verb preceded by the word *to* (to + verb). An infinitive can act as a noun, an adjective, or an adverb.

*George sat on the front step **to finish** his paper bird.*

Underline all of the infinitives in the directions for creating an origami bird.

1.
2.

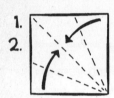

1. It is easy to create an origami bird, but you must be careful to follow the directions exactly.

2. To begin, you must cut out a perfect square (6" or about 15 cm) of paper. Then fold the outer edges to the middle on the dotted lines as shown.

3.

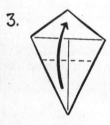

3. Now your paper should resemble a kite. Fold the "kite" in half in order to touch the top corner to the bottom corner.

4. Fold the tip down to form a beak.

4.

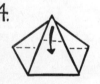

5. To continue, fold your paper back, as shown, on the dotted lines.

6. Your bird will begin to appear when you pull the beak out and the neck begins to move up at the same time.

7. Press the paper firmly at the stars to make the neck stay in place.

5.

8. It is important to fold the bottom points up on each side to add feet to your creation.

9. Try again by using different colors and sizes of paper to design dozens of origami birds.

6.

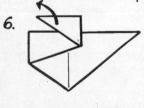

7.

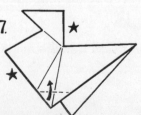

8.

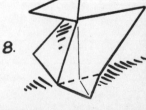

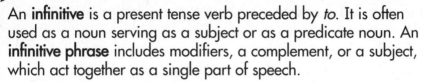

Cooking Up a Storm

infinitives and infinitive phrases

An **infinitive** is a present tense verb preceded by *to*. It is often used as a noun serving as a subject or as a predicate noun. An **infinitive phrase** includes modifiers, a complement, or a subject, which act together as a single part of speech.

> **subject**: *To make dinner* for Grandma was Lesley's reason for taking a cooking class.
>
> **predicate noun**: Lesley's hope is *to make a seven-course meal.*

Underline the infinitives or infinitive phrases in each of the following sentences.

1. To cook is my grandma's favorite hobby.
2. She likes to shop for interesting ingredients.
3. I was hoping to visit her after school.
4. One of my goals is to learn to make meatballs like Grandma's.
5. To make spaghetti is Grandma Elsie's specialty.
6. Her favorite kitchen experience is to create chocolate-covered cream puffs.

In each of the following sentences, underline the infinitive phrase used as a noun and indicate if it is a subject (**S**) or a predicate noun (**PN**).

_____ 1. To give a great party was Candy's plan.

_____ 2. To write the guest list was her first priority.

_____ 3. Her next step was to plan the menu and decorations.

_____ 4. Her idea was to celebrate with a Hawaiian theme.

_____ 5. To offer her guests grass skirts and leis seemed like a good idea.

_____ 6. To hula dance would also be a fun activity.

_____ 7. To view her work hours later gave her pleasure.

_____ 8. All that was left was to enjoy the party.

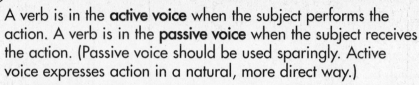

The Scavenger Hunt

active and passive voice verbs

A verb is in the **active voice** when the subject performs the action. A verb is in the **passive voice** when the subject receives the action. (Passive voice should be used sparingly. Active voice expresses action in a natural, more direct way.)

active voice: We played the scavenger hunt game at school.
passive voice: The scavenger hunt game was played by us at school.

Identify the verbs in the following sentences by labeling them **A** (active) or **P** (passive). If the verb is in passive voice, rewrite the sentence, changing the verb to active voice.

_____ 1. The scavenger hunt game was played by the entire class.

_____

_____

_____ 2. The class was divided into two teams by Mr. Mack, our homeroom teacher.

_____

_____

_____ 3. We called our team "The Scavengers."

_____

_____

_____ 4. The other team gave themselves the name "The Search Party."

_____

_____

_____ 5. All of the clues were carefully hidden by our teacher.

_____

_____

So Weird!

> An **irregular verb** is any verb that does not follow the *d* or *ed* pattern for forming the past tense and past participle.
>
> | | present | past | past participle |
> |---|---|---|---|
> | **regular verb** | jump | jumped | (have, has, had) jumped |
> | **irregular verb** | go | went | (have, has, had) gone |

For each of the irregular verbs below, write the missing forms.

Present	Past	Past Participle (have, has, or had)
think	thought	
spend		spent
	drove	driven
begin	began	
eat		eaten
fall	fell	
	hid	hidden
write		
	spoke	
hear		
		torn
	took	
weave		
	stole	
		chosen

Giant Pandas

A **linking verb** does not show action. It connects the subject of the sentence to a word or words in the predicate. Any verb that can be substituted by a form of *to be* is a linking verb.

(Pandas) **are** (enormous animals.)

(Ming Ling) **felt** (soft.)

In each of the following sentences, underline the linking verb and circle the words in the subject and the predicate that are joined (or connected) by it.

1. Giant pandas seem friendly and harmless.

2. They are very beautiful and look like cuddly teddy bears.

3. The giant panda is a native of the dense bamboo forests of China.

4. The Chinese people are extremely proud of pandas and have made them a symbol of their country.

5. Bamboo is the panda's primary food; it makes up almost 99 percent of the bear's diet.

6. Thousands of years ago, bamboo forests were bountiful in eastern China, and giant pandas dwelled there.

7. The biggest panda ever weighed was almost 400 pounds (182 kg), but the average panda weighs over 200 pounds (91 kg).

8. Panda cubs can be very small, weighing only about 5 ounces (140 g).

9. The bones of a panda are large, thick, and very heavy.

10. Pandas seem very happy in their lush, green habitat.

Mighty Minerals

subject complements

A **subject complement** is a word that comes after a linking verb and refers back to the subject. A noun used as a subject complement is called a **predicate noun.** When a pronoun is used, it is called a **predicate pronoun.** An adjective used as a subject complement is called a **predicate adjective**.

predicate noun: The ruby is a **gem**.
predicate pronoun: The ruby is *it*.
predicate adjective: The ruby is **red**.

In the following sentences, underline all of the subject complements. On the line, write **PN** for predicate noun, **PPN** for predicate pronoun, and **PA** for predicate adjective.

_____ 1. A person who studies minerals is a mineralogist.

_____ 2. Minerals are useful.

_____ 3. Minerals that make metals are ore minerals.

_____ 4. All minerals are uniquely beautiful.

_____ 5. Emeralds are green.

_____ 6. One very strong mineral is the diamond.

_____ 7. If you're looking for a very hard mineral, the diamond is it.

_____ 8. No mineral is harder.

_____ 9. Graphite, however, is very soft.

_____ 10. The black substance in a pencil that leaves a mark on paper is it.

_____ 11. One property of minerals is specific gravity.

_____ 12. Having a very high specific gravity, gold ore is extremely heavy.

_____ 13. The hobby of mineral collecting is popular.

Published by Instructional Fair. Copyright protected.   31   0-7424-0152-9 *Building Grammar*

Gone Fishin'

transitive and intransitive verbs

A **transitive verb** is an action verb that is followed by a direct object. The verb "transmits" the action from the subject to the object. An **intransitive verb** does not need an object to complete its meaning. It is frequently followed by a prepositional phrase.

transitive: We **caught** a fish.
intransitive: I **fish** with my dad.

In the spaces below, write **T** if the sentence contains a transitive verb; write **IT** if it contains an intransitive verb. Then underline the subject and the object (if one is present).

_____ 1. Live bait wiggles in the covered container.

_____ 2. I am wearing my new fishing hat.

_____ 3. Dad stocked the tackle box with all of our gear.

_____ 4. We packed a sack lunch of sandwiches and apples.

_____ 5. I prefer fishing in the boat.

_____ 6. Dad usually fishes from the pier.

_____ 7. We catch perch and catfish.

_____ 8. Our catch is placed in a wire mesh basket.

_____ 9. I don't mind baiting my own hook.

_____ 10. Before we head home, I want to catch a super big fish.

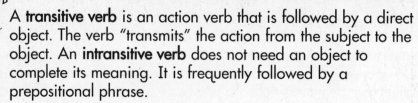

Published by Instructional Fair. Copyright protected.   32   0-7424-0152-9 *Building Grammar*

Duke's Dilemma

lie and lay

Lie means to recline, to rest, or to remain in a reclining position. The principal parts of *lie* are *lie, lay, (have, has, had) lain.* **Lay** means to put something down or to place something somewhere. Its principal parts are *lay, laid, (have, has, had) laid.* This verb always has an object.

lie: *His pets **lie** on the carpet waiting for him to arrive.*

lay: *When he arrives, he **lays** a treat for each of them on the floor.*

Circle the correct verb in each of the following sentences.

1. Fiffi meows happily when Mrs. McGregor (lays, lies) a bowl of milk in the corner.

2. While the cat enjoys the treat, Duke, the dog, (lays, lies) lazily on his rug in front of the fireplace.

3. Once, when Mrs. McGregor had (lain, laid) Duke's favorite rug in a different spot, the dog whimpered and growled for hours.

4. Fiffi (lay, laid) on the window seat meowing unhappily.

5. As soon as Mr. McGregor came home, he removed his shoes and (lay, laid) his hat on the table.

6. He noticed immediately that Duke was not (laying, lying) in his usual spot.

7. Mr. McGregor promptly (lay, laid) Duke's rug in its usual location.

8. A relieved Duke instantly (lay, laid) down and closed his eyes.

9. As for Fiffi, she was once again able to (lay, lie) peacefully on the window seat.

10. Mr. McGregor (laid, lay) in his recliner and watched the football game.

Published by Instructional Fair. Copyright protected.   33   0-7424-0152-9 *Building Grammar*

Set the Table, Sit for Tea

The verb **sit** means to assume a sitting position or to occupy a seat. The principal parts of *sit* are *sit, sat,* and *(have, has, had) sat.* The verb **set** means to put something in position or to make something rigid. The principal parts of *set* are *set, set,* and *(have, has, had) set.*

> **sit:** She likes to **sit** in the chair by the window.
> **set:** She **set** her tea on the ledge by the window.

Circle the correct verb in each of the following sentences.

1. Claire and I (sat, set) aside some time to spend with Mrs. Fargate, the widow who lives next door.

2. We had (sat, set) out our best clothes for the occasion.

3. When we arrived, Mrs. Fargate asked us to come in and (set, sit) down.

4. Several ceramic pots filled with coral-colored geraniums were (sat, set) on the window ledge to create a happy atmosphere.

5. I (sat, set) in an overstuffed chair with green-and-white checked cushions and looked around.

6. Claire chose to (set, sit) upon a fluffy couch.

7. Mrs. Fargate's miniature poodle, Teacup, (sat, set) politely on the rocking chair, showing off the pink ribbon attached to the curly hair on its forehead.

8. We (sat, set) there together talking about trivial things.

9. Mrs. Fargate (sat, set) out the dishes.

10. She served us frosted lemon bars, which she (sat, set) on lovely linen napkins.

11. Our hostess (sat, set) a fine white porcelain teapot, decorated with tiny painted roses, on the coffee table.

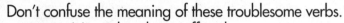

Accepting Exceptions

troublesome verbs

Don't confuse the meaning of these troublesome verbs.
accept: (v) to take what is offered
except: (prep) to leave out; other than
affect: (v) to influence; change
effect: (n) result; consequence

*We will **accept** the invitation.   The weather may **affect** our plans.*
*Everyone **except** Joe is going.   We hope the **effect** will be good.*

Circle the correct verb to complete each of the following sentences.

On the Beat

1. Police officers (accept, except) the responsibility of enforcing the law of the land.
2. Their commitment to the job can drastically (affect, effect) the community.
3. A policeman is a friend to everyone (accept, except) the lawbreaker.
4. Going to prison is one possible (affect, effect) of committing a crime.

Green Grass of Home

1. Yes, I am willing to (accept, except) payment for a job well done.
2. I always charge at least $10 when I mow a lawn, (accept, except) when I mow Mrs. Kennedy's for free.
3. Rain (affects, effects) how quickly the grass grows.
4. The (affect, effect) of lots of rain is a lot of lawn-mowing work for me.

A Good Example

1. I don't mind baby-sitting my little sister, (accept, except) when I have other plans.
2. Since she doesn't like anyone else to watch her, baby-sitting my sister has begun to (affect, effect) my social life.
3. My mom always tells me that I have a good (affect, effect) on my little sister.
4. I guess I can (accept, except) that.

Go Down, Moses

> A **direct object** is a noun, pronoun, or group of words acting as a noun that receives the action of the verb. It is easy to find the direct object by asking the question *what* or *whom* after the verb.
>
> *In seventh grade we study **heroes**.*
> Ask: We study **what**?   Answer: **heroes**

Read the sentences about Harriet Tubman and circle the direct objects. Some sentences may have one direct object, while other sentences may have none.

1. The courageous Harriet Tubman freed many slaves by way of the Underground Railroad.

2. The slaves would escape from the plantations in the middle of the night.

3. They desperately wanted freedom.

4. The band of fugitives traveled by foot from their southern states toward Canada.

5. Many brave men and women helped to hide the fugitives on their flight to freedom.

6. Fortunately, Harriet Tubman never lost any passengers on her nineteen trips on the Underground Railroad.

7. People offered rewards totaling $40,000 for the capture of Harriet Tubman.

8. As a spy during the Civil War, she freed more than 750 slaves.

9. Harriet Tubman risked her life to lead hundreds of men, women, and children to freedom.

Happily Ever After

An **indirect object** is a noun or pronoun that names the person *to whom* or *for whom* something is done. To find the indirect object, ask *to whom* or *for whom* after the action verb.

> The prince sang Cinderella an off-key love song.
> Question: The prince sang an off-key love song **to whom?**
> Answer: Cinderella

In each of the following sentences, underline the indirect object and circle the action verb.

1. She was bringing her grandmother a basket of goodies.

2. A man sold the little pig a bundle of sticks for building a house.

3. She left Baby Bear an empty porridge bowl.

4. They worked hard each night to make the shoemaker some leather shoes.

5. The wicked stepmother gave her many chores to do.

6. The pea hidden beneath the pile of mattresses gave her a sore back.

7. He handed his mother the magic beans.

8. The tailors made the emperor new royal garments.

9. She gave the wicked witch a push into the hot oven.

10. The handsome prince gave Sleeping Beauty a kiss to awaken her.

11. The wicked queen, dressed as an old hag, offered the girl a poisonous apple.

12. The tricky trio told the troll a lie.

Collection Craze

The noun or pronoun used as the **object of the preposition** follows the preposition or prepositional phrase. A preposition relates the noun or pronoun to another word in the sentence. To find the object of the preposition, ask *whom* or *what* after the preposition.

Lucinda jumped over the gate.
Lucinda jumped over what? **the gate**

Grandma sent money to us.
Grandma sent money to whom? **us**

Read the paragraphs below. Place parentheses around the prepositional phrases and underline the objects of the preposition.

It seems that everyone collects something these days. For some reason, collecting has become one of America's most popular hobbies. Aside from ordinary stamp or coin collecting, individuals of all ages are collecting everything from unique pencil erasers to the ever-popular stuffed animals. Baseball cards have been highly collectible for many years, but today a person can collect any kind of card, including basketball, football, hockey, and even postcards. Books, cars, shoes, teacups, hats—a collector's possibilities are endless.

Many people are willing to spend a great deal of money on their collections. A rare baseball card could cost a collector thousands of dollars. Doll collectors often spend hundreds of dollars for a single, yet desirable, piece for their collection. Without a doubt, these collectors hope that over many years their treasures will increase in value.

The World of Greek Mythology

A **prepositional phrase** is a group of words that shows how two words or ideas are related to each other. It can function as an adjective or an adverb, depending on the word it modifies. Like a one-word adjective, an **adjective prepositional phrase** modifies only a noun or a pronoun.

*One ancient myth **about the rainbow goddess named Iris** captivated my attention.*

In the following sentences, underline the adjective prepositional phrases and draw an arrow to the word being modified. Make sure the prepositional phrase modifies a noun.

1. Ancient Greek stories about gods and goddesses are called myths.

2. Myths from the Greek world were created to explain the mysteries of nature.

3. Poseidon, god of the sea, was also god of earthquakes and horses.

4. The world of mythology is filled with gods, goddesses, and mortals with many marvelous powers.

5. The *Iliad* and the *Odyssey*, by Homer, contain most of the main mythological characters and themes.

6. Eros, from ancient mythology, assisted many in their quest for love.

7. Mount Olympus was the home of the major Greek gods and goddesses.

8. Zeus was a powerful Olympian in the sky and ruled over all the gods.

9. Aphrodite was known as the goddess of love and beauty.

10. Hades' home in the underworld was the land of the dead.

11. Apollo was very strong and was known as the god of music, poetry, and purity.

12. Messages for the gods were delivered by Hermes, who was swift of flight.

The White House

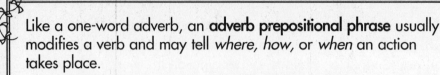

> Like a one-word adverb, an **adverb prepositional phrase** usually modifies a verb and may tell *where, how,* or *when* an action takes place.
>
> *The White House is located* **in Washington, D.C.**
> (tells where)
> *The president resides there* **with his family members**. (tells how)
> *He will leave the White House* **at the end of his term**.
> (tells when)

In the following sentences, underline the adverb prepositional phrases. At the end of each sentence, write whether it tells **where**, **how**, or **when** the action takes place.

1. The West Wing was completed in 1909 and includes the new oval office.

2. Since 1934, the Oval Office has served as the president's formal office.

3. The president and the first lady entertain guests in the East Room.

4. Inside the Green Room, which he used as a dining area, Thomas Jefferson placed a green cloth on the floor.

5. The Green Room became a sitting room when it was decorated with green furnishings.

6. The Blue Room was named by Martin Van Buren, the eighth president.

7. The nineteenth-century president Rutherford B. Hayes took the oath of office in the Red Room, which is used today as a sitting room.

8. Before state dinners, the president often entertains foreign leaders in the Yellow Oval Room.

9. In 1941, the executive wing replaced a greenhouse complex.

10. In the Lincoln Bedroom, the Emancipation Proclamation was signed by President Lincoln.

Who's Better?

comparative and superlative degrees of adjectives and adverbs

A **comparative adjective** or **adverb** is used to describe a comparison between two things, people, places, or actions. A **superlative adjective** or **adverb** compares three or more things, people, places, or actions.

	positive	*comparative*	*superlative*
adjectives	*happy*	*happier*	*happiest*
	good	*better*	*best*
adverbs	*happily*	*more/less happily*	*most/least happily*
	well	*better*	*best*

Add the comparative and superlative forms of each adjective and adverb in the charts below.

Adjectives

Positive	Comparative	Superlative
new		
durable		
cheap		
big		
comfortable		
beautiful		
creative		

Adverbs

Positive	Comparative	Superlative
proudly		
courageously		
quickly		
easily		
cheerfully		
safely		
slowly		

Touring the Zoo

> **This**, **that**, **these**, and **those** are adjectives that modify nouns by telling *which one* or *which ones*. *This* and *that* are singular. *These* and *those* are plural. *This* and *these* refer to things nearby, and *that* and *those* refer to things farther away.
>
> **This** *zoo we are visiting is the best in the state.*
> **That** *zoo across town isn't nearly as nice.*
> **These** *animals we are seeing are cared for very well.*
> **Those** *animals over there are not cared for very well.*

Circle the correct form of each adjective in the following sentences.

1. To your immediate right you will see (this, these) beautiful pink flamingos.

2. Just past the trees are (these, those) peacocks displaying their elaborately decorated tail feathers.

3. (That, This) bald eagle nesting in the exhibit next to you has recently hatched an eaglet.

4. Here inside this building we see (these, those) handsome penguins swimming in the frigid water.

5. Over there you will see (these, those) marvelous white polar bears resting on the ice.

6. Right in front of you is (this, these) special sea lion and her cub.

7. Let's head back outside to see (these, those) fantastic big cats.

8. Here we see (this, these) sleeping lions.

9. Farther down the path are (these, those) pacing tigers.

10. And way over there is (this, that) breathtaking snow leopard.

Get Your Popcorn Here!

> *This, that, these,* and *those* are **demonstrative adjectives** that point out a particular person, place, or thing. Use *this* and *these* for things close by and *that* and *those* for things distant in time or space. *This* and *that* are singular while *these* and *those* are plural.

Underline the demonstrative adjectives and the words they modify.

1. I'd like some of this cotton candy, please.
2. I'm not interested in those bags of peanuts.
3. Could you help me carry these cups of soda?
4. This pack of gummy pandas will keep my little brother happy.
5. Please grab that box of chocolates for me.
6. Look at those huge buckets of popcorn!
7. Before we sit down, I think I'll take that box of spiced candy.
8. I think we should share these candy bars.

> An **indefinite adjective** is an adjective that gives an approximate number or quantity or that refers to no specific person or thing. It does not tell exactly how many or how much.
>
> *When we go out, we buy a few snacks to share with each other.*

In the following sentences, underline the indefinite adjectives.

1. When many friends go to the theater with me, we buy more snacks and pass them around.
2. Each person in the group buys something different to pass.
3. Some friends choose candy.
4. Of course, many people prefer to buy salty snacks to eat.
5. Soda pop is usually purchased by several movie goers.
6. After the movie, all snackers feel a little sick.

Spelunking

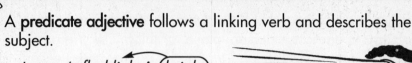

A **predicate adjective** follows a linking verb and describes the subject.

*Lanora's flashlight **is** bright.*

In each of the following sentences, underline the linking verb and circle the predicate adjective(s). Then draw an arrow from the predicate adjective to the subject it modifies.

1. The cave was cold and damp.

2. Deep inside the cave it was pitch dark, and we had to use flashlights to see where we were going.

3. Although a litter of bats hanging above us was intimidating, none came near us.

4. The stalactites overhead were wet.

5. They were shiny and beautiful, like icicles.

6. The stalagmites growing out of the cave floor were equally amazing.

7. Droplets of water falling into the nearby pools were surprisingly noisy in the quiet cave.

8. Several areas of the cave were still unexplored.

9. Our tour was very informative.

For each illustration below, write a sentence containing a subject, a linking verb, and a predicate adjective.

1. _____

_____

2. _____

_____

A Really Bad Beginning

good and well, bad and badly

> **Good** and **bad** are adjectives that modify nouns. **Well** and **badly** are adverbs that modify verbs.
>
> *That was a **good** shot.* (adjective)
> *He shot **well**.* (adverb)
> *That was a **bad** shot.* (adjective)
> *He shot **badly**.* (adverb)

Select the correct modifier in each of the following sentences.

When I woke up this morning I was feeling quite (good, well). I went to the sink to give my teeth a (good, well) brushing, but when I glanced in the mirror, I saw it. There, on my forehead, was a huge red pimple, and it looked really (bad, badly). I tried combing my bangs straight down over the ugly thing, but that didn't work too (good, well). Then I tried sticking a round bandage over it, but that didn't look very (good, well) either.

Maybe I could pop it, I thought, but decided that I might hurt myself too (bad, badly). A (good, well) cover-up might work. So next I tried my mom's make-up stick, which worked pretty (good, well), if you consider a big brown bump in the middle of your fore-head a (good, well) thing. As a last resort, I threw on my favorite hat, which hid the nasty zit fairly (good, well). The (bad, badly) thing is that hats aren't allowed in any of my classes. I wished so (bad, badly) that I could just stay home. I had a feeling it wasn't going to be a very (good, well) day at all.

A Close Call

Adverbs have three degrees of comparison. They are positive, comparative, and superlative. Some adverbs form the comparative degree by adding **er** and the superlative degree by adding **est**. Most adverbs that end in *ly* form their comparative degrees by adding the words **more** or **less** in front of the positive degree. The superlative degree is formed by adding the words **most** or **least** in front of the positive degree.

Raquel danced less gracefully than her sisters.
I hope they will come sooner rather than later.

Write the missing adverbs in the chart.

Positive	Comparative	Superlative
fast	faster	fastest
carefully	more/less carefully	most/least carefully
soon		
hard		
noisily		
late		
easily		
efficiently		
loudly		
softly		
harshly		
neatly		
cheerfully		
courageously		
correctly		

Negative Norman

A **double negative** incorrectly uses two negative words when one is sufficient. Use only one negative when you mean to say "no."

Noelle didn't want no macaroni. (incorrect)
Noelle didn't want any macaroni. (correct)

Rewrite each sentence so that it does not contain a double negative.

1. Negative Norman never seems to like nothing.

   _____

   _____

2. On Saturday mornings when his mom makes him pancakes, he says, "I don't want none!"

   _____

   _____

3. When his buddies from school call, he will not talk to no one.

   _____

   _____

4. Norman is so nasty he won't even feed his dog no food.

   _____

   _____

5. All day he just sits in his beanbag chair and won't never go nowhere.

   _____

   _____

6. Norman doesn't seem to have no smile at all.

   _____

   _____

7. He obviously hasn't learned nothing about enjoying life.

   _____

   _____

Ancient Pyramids

sentences with modifiers

> The complete subject or complete predicate of a sentence usually contains words or phrases called **modifiers** that add to the meaning of the sentence.
>
> *The ancient tombs, **which stand powerfully on the hot sands of Egypt**, are an amazing and wonderful sight.*

In the following sentences, underline the subject modifiers once and the predicate modifiers twice.

1. Ancient pyramids stand majestically in the golden desert sands of Egypt.

2. The Egyptian pyramids were erected nearly five thousand years ago.

3. Skilled craftsmen and unskilled laborers worked together to build the pyramids.

4. Brilliant architects carefully calculated and thoughtfully designed the pyramids.

5. The dangerous, difficult work of building pyramids was done slowly and carefully.

6. These incredibly large structures were built especially for the pharaohs.

7. Ancient Egyptians believed wholeheartedly in life after death.

8. The bodies of dead kings were effectively preserved and buried in the tombs.

Locked Out

misplaced modifiers

Modifiers that are not placed near the words or phrases that they modify are called **misplaced modifiers**.

Scared to death, the black night enveloped the lost student. (misplaced modifier)

Scared to death, the lost student wandered the neighborhood frantically. (correct)

Underline the misplaced modifiers in the following sentences. Then rewrite each sentence correctly.

1. After school, I have a key for getting into our locked house.

_____

2. Under the flower pot I always know I can find an extra key.

_____

3. The flower pot is missing unfortunately.

_____

4. In the basement, I consider breaking a window.

_____

5. On the roof, I think about going down the chimney.

_____

6. Instead, I sit on the porch and wait for my mom to get home for an hour.

_____

Sand and Surf

> If a modifying word, phrase, or clause does not modify a
> particular word, then it is called a **dangling modifier**. Every
> modifier must have a word that it clearly modifies.
>
> *Warmed by the sun, it felt good to be at the beach.*
> *(dangling modifier—"Warmed by the sun" does not*
> *modify "it")*
> *Warmed by the sun, we relaxed on our beach towels.*
> *(correct—"Warmed by the sun" does modify "we")*

Rewrite these sentences, correcting the dangling modifiers.

1. Riding the big waves, excited shouts emerge from the water.

   _____

   _____

2. Lying in the sun, my suntan lotion didn't work.

   _____

   _____

3. Playing barefoot, the volleyball game took place on the hot sand.

   _____

   _____

4. Tired and sandy, our beach day ended.

   _____

   _____

5. Hanging out at the beach, the time was a lot of fun.

   _____

   _____

Star-Crossed Lovers

participles and participial phrases

> A **participle** is a verb form that can function as an adjective.
> The **present participle** is usually formed by adding *ing* to a
> present tense verb. The **past participle** is usually formed by
> adding *ed* to the present tense. A **participial phrase** is a group
> of words that includes the participle and its objects, comple-
> ments, or modifiers.
>
> **present participle:** *Rex barks at the **passing** cars.*
> **past participle:** *A **determined** Rex tried to chase the car.*

In each of the following sentences, identify whether the participle used is a
present (**P**) or a past (**PA**) participle.

_____ 1. Romeo's parents inquire about their moping son.

_____ 2. The conniving Benvolio encourages Romeo to "crash" the
Capulet party.

_____ 3. A masked Romeo arrives at the party.

_____ 4. There he sees the smiling Juliet and longs to meet her.

_____ 5. The dancing couple fall hopelessly in love.

_____ 6. Love struck Juliet is distressed to learn that Romeo belongs
to the house of Montague.

_____ 7. The feuding Montagues and Capulets hate each other.

_____ 8. Juliet declares her passion for her dashing hero.

_____ 9. Her words of love inspire the snooping Romeo.

_____ 10. Soon, a determined Romeo appeals to the friar to marry
the couple immediately.

_____ 11. The young lovers are married in secret before a robed
friar.

Chores

A **gerund** is a verb form ending in *ing* that functions as a noun. Gerunds are formed by adding *ing* to the present tense verb form. A **gerund phrase** is a group of words that includes a gerund and its related words.

> **gerund**: *Dancing* is my favorite form of exercise.
> **gerund phrase**: *Dancing the polka* is a good workout.

In each of the following sentences, underline the gerund or gerund phrase and indicate how it is being used in the sentence: **S** (subject), **DO** (direct object), **OP** (object of a preposition), or **PN** (predicate noun).

_____ 1. Cleaning is the worst job.

_____ 2. I prefer cooking.

_____ 3. Sometimes I avoid my chores by complaining.

_____ 4. Another strategy is procrastinating.

_____ 5. Vacuuming isn't so bad.

_____ 6. I hate dusting.

_____ 7. Occasionally, the windows need washing.

_____ 8. Mopping makes the floors shine.

_____ 9. My room appears messy when the bed needs making.

_____ 10. Mowing the lawn can be relaxing work.

_____ 11. I'm not fond of pulling weeds when it's scorching hot outside.

_____ 12. Washing dishes is a job my sister and I share.

_____ 13. A disgusting chore is scrubbing the toilet.

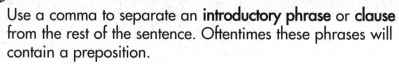

Medieval Times

> Use a comma to separate an **introductory phrase** or **clause** from the rest of the sentence. Oftentimes these phrases will contain a preposition.
>
> *Because I am sick, I will not be able to attend the medieval festival at the park.*

Underline the introductory phrase or clause in each of the following sentences. Then add the proper punctuation to each one.

1. During the Middle Ages the European form of government was feudalism.

2. At that time in European history there were many fiefs, estates of feudal lords.

3. In return for his loyalty a nobleman was provided with land by the king.

4. Under the feudal system the owner of a fief was often a lord whose land was inhabited by people who promised to serve him.

5. When a person controlled land he also had political, economic, judicial, and military power.

6. At the age of about seven many young boys left home to train for knighthood.

7. As soon as a squire had mastered the necessary skills he became a knight.

8. As a knight a nobleman was a soldier for the king when necessary.

9. Because they had few rights peasants were at the mercy of their lords.

10. In return for clerical services many lords gave fiefs to the church.

At the Carnival

> An **independent clause** is a group of words with a subject and
> a predicate that expresses a complete thought and can stand
> by itself as a sentence. A **dependent clause** cannot stand alone.
> It depends upon the independent clause of the sentence to
> complete its meaning. Dependent clauses start with words like
> *who, which, that, because, when, if, until, before,* and *after.*
>
>   **dependent**   **independent**
> *When we went to the school carnival, we witnessed many
> pranks.*

Match independent clauses to dependent clauses to form new sentences.

1. The teacher fell into the dunk tank

2. Her face turned bright red

3. The pie hit her in the face

4. After he fell asleep,

5. All the girls screamed

6. He was so embarrassed

7. They put a worm on his plate

8. Everyone laughed

— because she had a "kick-
me" sign stuck to her back.
— after their canoe was tipped
over.
— when the baseball hit the
target.
— they sprayed shaving cream
all over his head.
— while he was not looking.
— when she saw her undies
being strung up the flagpole.
— that he couldn't speak.
— when he threw it.

The sentences below each have a dependent and an independent clause.
Underline the dependent clause once and the independent clause twice.

1. Janie was sad because she didn't have enough money to go on the
   Ferris wheel.

2. After Jack ate two bags of cotton candy, he felt sick.

3. While Mrs. Brown wasn't looking, two kids snuck into the Tunnel O' Love.

4. The girls all cheered when the carnival strongman lifted two grown
   men over his head.

Window-Washing Entrepreneurs

A **noun clause** is a dependent clause that functions as a noun. It may be used as a subject, a direct object, an indirect object, an object of a preposition, or a predicate noun.

subject: **What occurred** was not planned at all.
direct object: They wondered **what they should do** now.
indirect object: Should they make **whoever broke the window** pay the bill?
object of the preposition: They were grateful to **whoever would clean up the mess.**
predicate noun: The good thing was **that no one was hurt.**

In each of the following sentences, underline the noun clause and indicate how the clause is used in the sentence: **S** (subject), **DO** (direct object), **IO** (indirect object), **OP** (object of a preposition), or **PN** (predicate noun).

_____ 1. Felix and Frank considered what they could do to earn money.

_____ 2. Felix thought that his idea might work.

_____ 3. What Felix proposed was to start their own window-washing business.

_____ 4. That people would want their windows cleaned seemed obvious to Frank.

_____ 5. How to get the proper equipment was what they had to figure out first.

_____ 6. Whatever they could promise to persuade their customers, they printed in their advertisement fliers.

_____ 7. They would give whoever called in the first week a discount price.

_____ 8. Felix and Frank agreed that the fliers should be hand-delivered.

Masterpiece in the Snow

An **adjective clause** is a dependent clause that functions as an adjective by telling *what kind* or *which one*. An **adverb clause** is a dependent clause that functions as an adverb. It can modify verbs, adjectives, or other adverbs and tells *where, when, in what manner, to what extent, under what condition,* or *why*. A **noun clause** is a dependent clause that functions as a noun.

> **adjective clause**: *Building a snowman is one pastime **that we enjoy each winter.***
>
> **adverb clause**: *We dress warmly **when we play in the snow.***
> **noun clause**: ***What we create out of the snow** is always a labor of love.*

In each of the following sentences, underline the dependent clause and indicate if it is an adjective (**ADJ**), an adverb (**ADV**), or a noun (**N**) clause.

_____ 1. We didn't want to build a snowman that was like all the others.

_____ 2. Today we would create a snowman that no one would forget.

_____ 3. What Craig thought of was perfect!

_____ 4. Build a giant snow monster is what we would do.

_____ 5. The monster grew quickly because the snow packed so well.

_____ 6. The neighbor who lives next door brought a six-foot ladder.

_____ 7. What became the monster's body were packed, giant snowballs.

_____ 8. He grew taller after we hoisted the second ball on top of the first.

_____ 9. To build his height, we added buckets of snow.

So Many Sweets

Noun Clauses

Underline the noun clause and indicate how the clause is being used in the sentence: **S** (subject), **DO** (direct object), **IO** (indirect object), **OP** (object of the preposition), or **PN** (predicate noun).

_____ 1. Frosted cookies are what make Christmas delicious.

_____ 2. Whoever made this chocolate pie should be kissed.

_____ 3. I hope that this caramel corn isn't stale.

_____ 4. Meg will give whoever says please a giant candy bar.

_____ 5. She shoved cotton candy into whatever space she could find in her mouth.

Adjective Clauses

In each of the following sentences, underline the adjective clause and circle the word it modifies.

1. We buy ice cream from the man who drives the ice-cream truck.

2. The honey that the bees make tastes great on toast.

3. His jawbreaker, which was the size of a golf ball, lasted a long time.

4. Dad and I get doughnuts at the bakery where my cousin works.

5. The fudge maker who worked in town was known for his delicious candy.

Adverb Clauses

In each of the following sentences, underline the adverb clause and write the question it answers: *how, when, where,* or *why.*

_____ 1. You should brush your teeth whenever you've eaten sweets.

_____ 2. My brother is hyperactive because he ate too much Halloween candy.

_____ 3. At Christmastime, we dip candy canes in melted chocolate.

_____ 4. We fondue by dipping strawberries in melted chocolate, too.

_____ 5. Lisa and Mike shared a malted milk shake at the ice-cream parlor.

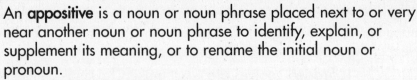

A Bag of Bones

An **appositive** is a noun or noun phrase placed next to or very near another noun or noun phrase to identify, explain, or supplement its meaning, or to rename the initial noun or pronoun.

Bones, _**the scaffolding of the body**_, are tied together with ligaments.

Underline the appositives in each sentence. There may be more than one appositive in each.

1. The cranium, or brain case, is made up of five bones.

2. The clavicle, or collarbone, is a slender, rodlike bone that acts like a brace for the shoulder blade.

3. The shoulder blades, or scapulae, are broad, triangle-shaped bones located on either side of the upper back.

4. A person's breastbone, the sternum, is a flat, elongated bone.

5. Each upper limb of a person's body consists of an upper arm bone, the humerus, and two lower arm bones, the radius and the ulna.

6. Your wrist, or carpus, is composed of eight small carpal bones that are firmly connected in two rows of four bones each.

7. Phlanges, finger and toe bones, play an important role in the body.

8. While in-line skating, John hurt his patella, his kneecap, when he collided with a parked car.

9. The lower leg is formed by two bones, the large tibia and the slender fibula, which extend from the knee to the ankle.

10. The longest bone in the body, the femur, extends from the hip to the knee.

A Sour Experience

simple subject and predicate

> The **simple subject** names the person or the object the sentence is about, not including modifying words such as articles (a, an, the) or adjectives. The **simple predicate** tells what the subject is or what the subject does. It is a verb or a verb phrase minus any modifying words.
>
> (simple subject) ↘   ↙ (simple predicate)
> A happy <u>kid</u> <u>munched</u> on sour apples.
>
> (simple subject) ↘   ↙ (simple predicate)
> <u>Mrs. Haggly</u> <u>is taking</u> the apple trees away.

Read the story. Underline the simple subject and circle the simple predicate in each sentence.

The apple trees along Mrs. Haggly's driveway tempted us. From our own yard, we could smell the tartness in the crisp autumn air. Shiny green apples decorated the gnarled old trees. We strained our necks to see them better. Just the thought of biting into one of those apples made our mouths water uncontrollably.

Mrs. Haggly was our only problem. Everyone knew that she was dangerous. She had long, wavy white hair and a crooked face. She bent over, using a cane for balance. Many people thought she might even be a witch.

One morning, we decided to make a run for the apples. Boy was that exciting! My brother ran first. I followed. Before we knew it, we had a handful of perfect little green apples. Back over the fence we went, quicker than ever! Exhausted and sweating beads of fear, we ate the green apples under the shade of our own tree. They were perfectly sour and delicious!

However, we paid the price for our adventure. Ohhh, did we ache! Our stomachs grew big like watermelons. We were sick all day. This story has a moral. Little green apples are sometimes wicked. Old ladies with canes are usually not.

Autumn and Apples

compound subject and predicate

A **compound subject** is made of two or more subjects that have the same verb and are joined by a conjunction such as *and* or *or*. A **compound predicate** is two or more predicates that have the same subject and are joined by a conjunction.

(compound subject) ↘   ↙ (compound predicate)

My sister **and** I _love to make **and** eat caramel apples_.

Underline the compound portion in each of the following sentences. Write **CS** in the blank if it is a compound subject; write **CP** if it is a compound predicate.

____   1.   In the fall, my sister and I always make caramel apples.

____   2.   First, we pick the apples and wash them well.

____   3.   Then, Tami and I melt the caramel squares in the double boiler.

____   4.   If we do not stir the caramels well enough, the mixture will be too chunky and will not work.

____   5.   While we work, Kenneth, our younger brother, eats an apple or sneaks some caramels.

____   6.   Finally, Tami starts dipping and turning the first apple in the hot caramel.

____   7.   Mom and Dad like chopped nuts on their apples.

____   8.   I roll a few apples in the nuts and leave some plain.

____   9.   After dinner, our family will devour and enjoy them for dessert.

____   10. We love to make caramel apples but hate to clean up the sticky mess and put away all the dishes.

Homework

There are four kinds of sentences: **declarative**, **interrogative**, **imperative**, and **exclamatory**.

- **Declarative** sentences make a statement and end with a period.
- **Interrogative** sentences ask a question and end with a question mark.
- **Imperative** sentences command or make a request and end with a period or an exclamation point. ("You" is the implied subject of the command or request.)
- **Exclamatory** sentences make either a statement or a command with strong feeling and end with exclamation points.

Label the following sentences: **D** (declarative), **IN** (interrogative), **IM** (imperative), or **E** (exclamatory). Add the correct punctuation to the end of each sentence.

_____ 1. My teachers always give me too much homework

_____ 2. Don't they know I already have enough to do

_____ 3. Mow the lawn

_____ 4. That's what my dad always says

_____ 5. Did you take out the trash

_____ 6. My mom always wants me to empty the trash cans and take them out to the curb

_____ 7. Sometimes I even have to help my brother with his paper route

_____ 8. Just imagine how tired I get

_____ 9. Can't a guy get a break

_____ 10. Mrs. Barts wants me to do a report about Egyptian mummies, and Mr. Lee suggests I study for the algebra test

_____ 11. What do I know about mummies anyway

0-7424-0152-9 *Building Grammar*

Sumo

simple and compound sentences

A **simple sentence** contains one independent clause. (An independent clause contains a subject and a predicate and can stand alone.) A **compound sentence** contains two independent clauses that are closely related. A comma and conjunction or a semicolon usually connects the two clauses.

> *Maxwell is a sumo wrestler. (simple sentence)*
> *Maxwell trains very hard, but he has never won a competition. (compound sentence)*

Put an **S** on the line in front of each simple sentence and a **C** on the line in front of each compound sentence.

_____ 1. Sumo is the national sport of Japan.

_____ 2. There are six major sumo tournaments held each year in Japan, and they attract the attention of the entire nation.

_____ 3. In Japan, a tournament is called a *basho*.

_____ 4. A sumo ring measures 12 feet (3.66 m) in diameter and is made of sand and clay.

_____ 5. The goal in sumo wrestling is to either throw your opponent to the ground or to force him out of the ring.

_____ 6. Sumo has no weight classes for competition, and many wrestlers weigh more than 350 pounds (159 kg).

_____ 7. The wrestler's big stomach provides him a low center of gravity, and it helps him withstand a charge by his opponent.

_____ 8. Every sumo competition begins with a religious-type ceremony.

_____ 9. Before each match, the competitors clap their hands to awaken the gods, they throw salt into the ring to purify the ground, and they stamp their feet to crush evil.

_____ 10. When the referee gives the signal, the wrestlers take their positions.

Butterflies

A **complex sentence** contains an independent clause and one or more dependent clauses. An **independent clause** contains a subject and a predicate and can stand alone. A **dependent clause** has a subject and a predicate, but it cannot stand by itself and still make sense. A dependent clause often begins with a relative pronoun such as *who, which, that, whose,* or *whom.*

> **independent clause**: *The butterfly flitted from flower to flower.*
>
> **dependent clause**: *whose wings were brightly colored*
>
> **complex sentence**: *The butterfly, whose wings were brightly colored, flitted from flower to flower.*

Underline the dependent clauses in the sentences below.

1. The butterfly, which is a cousin to the moth, can be seen near flower beds during the day.

2. Butterflies, whose bodies are partly covered with multicolored scales, have six legs, four wings, and two antennae.

3. Because of its many rows of scales, the butterfly has beautifully colored wings with fantastic designs.

4. The eye of a butterfly, which is made up of thousands of tiny lenses, sees color and movement very well.

5. The two antennae, which are located on the top of its head, are the smell sensors of the butterfly.

6. Because the butterfly is often in search of nectar, it flies from flower to flower.

7. While it searches for nectar, the butterfly performs an important job.

8. It carries pollen from one flower to another, which helps the flowers reproduce.

Who Am I?

A **compound-complex sentence** contains two or more independent clauses and at least one dependent clause.

When you read the clues, you will begin to identify the mystery animal, and you will make your guess.

In these compound-complex sentences, underline the independent clauses once and the dependent clauses twice. Can you guess what animal this is?

1. Because the weather is turning cold, I will go south, and I will join others like myself.

2. I can weigh more than ten elephants, and when I am fully grown, my length is greater than a four-story building.

3. Scientists, who are called cetologists, know we have black and white markings, but our markings differ from one another.

4. Though we all have similar markings, our individual ones are just as unique as a person's fingerprints, and they are as individual as a giraffe's spots.

5. I have a big tail, and I like to flip it up when I am traveling.

6. My skin, which covers my entire body, is smooth and hairless, but it is bumpy on parts of my head.

7. Although I eat huge amounts of food, I have no teeth, instead I have baleens.

8. If I rise out of the water, you might see my dorsal fins, or I might show you a glimpse of my tail.

9. Underneath my skin is a thick layer of dense fatty tissue, which is called blubber, and it maintains my body temperature at 93° to 99° F (34° to 37° C).

Soup's On

A **simple sentence** contains one independent clause. A **compound sentence** is made of two independent clauses connected by a comma and conjunction. A **complex sentence** includes one independent clause and one or more dependent clauses. A **compound-complex sentence** contains two or more independent clauses (connected by a comma and conjunction) and at least one dependent clause.

simple: I like soup.
compound: I like soup, and I prefer it hot.
complex: When I get home from school, I like soup.
compound-complex: When I get home from school, I like soup, and I prefer it hot.

Identify the following sentences as **S** (simple), **C** (compound), **CX** (complex), or **C-CX** (compound-complex).

_____ 1. My grandma makes the best cheesy broccoli soup, and she serves it with homemade bread.

_____ 2. Big chunks of potatoes make potato soup worth eating.

_____ 3. Even though I hate pea soup, my mom always makes it.

_____ 4. Chili tastes great on a cold winter day.

_____ 5. Because we eat soup every Saturday night, we try lots of kinds, and we serve them in a variety of ways.

_____ 6. When we go out for Chinese food, we usually order egg drop soup.

_____ 7. In my opinion, a black bean soup with a rice and tomato salsa on top is the ultimate best.

_____ 8. If you come over tonight, you may stay for dinner, and we will share our minestrone.

_____ 9. Dad loves venison stew and whole wheat rolls.

_____ 10. Some people like clam chowder, but I'm not crazy about it.

The Rodeo

A group of words punctuated like a sentence but not containing a complete thought is called a **fragment**.

fragment: *One of the reasons I could not do my homework.*
correct: *One of the reasons I could not do my homework is that I went to the rodeo.*

Correct each of the fragments by connecting it to a "partner" sentence or group of words. Write the correct letter on the line. If the sentence is not a fragment, write **OK** on the line.

A. bareback riders use

B. entertain the crowd

C. untamed horses

D. great North American sport

E. doesn't use a saddle

F. bull riding

G. he gets bucked off

H. is thrilling

____ 1. A bareback bronco rider.

____ 2. For over 150 years, rodeo has been a.

____ 3. At the rodeo, bucking broncos and their riders.

____ 4. Riders mount in a stall called a chute.

____ 5. A leather handle called a rigging to hang on to.

____ 6. The eight second ride.

____ 7. The cowboy tries to stay on the horse.

____ 8. Will try to toss riders off.

____ 9. Then the pick-up man helps.

____ 10. Is truly the most dangerous event.

____ 11. If he can't hang on.

____ 12. A clown distracts it.

By the Shore

A **run-on sentence** consists of two or more complete sentences written without proper punctuation between them. Run-ons can be corrected in three ways.

1. If the two sentences are closely related, they can be separated by a semicolon.

   Shells are very pretty; they make especially good necklaces.

2. Closely related sentences can also be separated with a comma and a conjunction.

   I like all kinds of fish, but angel fish are my favorite.

3. Sentences that are not closely related can be separated with a period.

   Puffer fish are funny-looking. They live in salt water.

Correct the run-ons below by adding the proper punctuation and conjunctions if necessary. If a sentence is not a run-on, write **OK** on the line.

_____ 1. The moray eel conceals himself by hiding in the rocks he pops his head out to catch his prey.

_____ 2. A group of sea animals named sea squirts shoot water through one of two body openings.

_____ 3. Starfish and sea urchins have no head they have mouths on their bellies.

_____ 4. Starfish have five flexible arms they use them to walk around.

_____ 5. A seahorse is a fish that swims in an upright position the male has a kangaroo-like pouch that holds the fertilized eggs until they hatch.

_____ 6. Most sea urchins are vegetarians or scavengers most are equipped with five sharp teeth for scraping food.

_____ 7. Sand dollars are shallow-water echinoderms their bodies are covered with spines which aid in locomotion.

_____ 8. Seaweed is commonly found along rocky beaches because it grows attached to the rocks.

Prehistoric Creatures

Use **hyphens** to
  a. break a word between syllables at the end of a line in running text.
  b. join two-part numbers from twenty-one to ninety-nine.
  c. write a fraction as a word.
  d. join some compound nouns and adjectives.

  a. Some scientists claim that dino-
  saurs roamed the earth millions of years ago.
  b. thirty-five, eighty-two
  c. one-fortieth, two-thirds
  d. fat-necked, hurricane-like

Add a hyphen to each of the following sentences. Then, in the blank, write the letter from above to show which rule you have applied.

_____ 1. The woolly mammoth was an elephant like animal covered with long, thick hair.

_____ 2. The mammoths had long, curved tusks useful dur ing the winter in clearing away the snow to find grass to eat.

_____ 3. In permafrost regions of Siberia, some mam moths have been found perfectly preserved.

_____ 4. The average Stegosaurus was twenty five feet long and weighed two to three tons.

_____ 5. The four sharp spikes on its tail were quite use ful in wounding its enemies.

_____ 6. Triceratops, meaning "three horned face," was an aggressive dinosaur.

_____ 7. It chewed large amounts of plants with its razor sharp teeth.

_____ 8. Triceratops stood nine and one half feet tall.

_____ 9. Tyrannosaurus, a forty seven foot tyrant, weighed seven tons.

Gossip

> A **direct quotation** is the use of someone's exact words. It is always set off with quotation marks. An **indirect quotation** is the writer's description of someone else's words. It does not require quotation marks.
>
> **direct**: Brent said, "Max is bringing the dog to the vet."
> **indirect**: Brent said that Max is bringing the dog to the vet.

For each of the following sentences, write **DQ** (direct quotation) or **IQ** (indirect quotation) on the line. Then add quotation marks where they are needed.

The Orange Hair

____ 1. Jennifer asked, Did you see Rae's hair? It's bright orange!

____ 2. She dyed it herself, said Jordan.

____ 3. Yeah, Tamara said with a sneer, she needs a wig.

The Surprise Party

____ 1. I'll see you at the party, declared Paige.

____ 2. What party? asked Maya.

____ 3. Steve's brothers are giving him a surprise birthday party, answered Paige, and everyone is going.

____ 4. Maya said that she would love to go, too.

The Joke

____ 1. Don't look now, warned Jeff, but Robby is about to drink his pop.

____ 2. So what? Anna asked.

____ 3. Dan told Anna about the plastic worm that they had dropped in Robby's cup.

____ 4. Jeff then said that Robby had just spit his pop across the table.

In the Pool!

> A **colon** is used between the hour and the minutes when time is written using numbers. A **colon** is also used to introduce a list or a series of things unless the series is preceded by an expression such as, *for example, namely, for instance,* or *that is.*
>
> *School begins at 8:20 A.M. each day, Monday through Friday.*
>
> *I have to take several things to school each day: my backpack, my lunch, and my house key.*
>
> *I have to take several things to school each day, namely, my backpack, my lunch, and my house key.*

Write the time correctly in the blanks using numbers and colons.

_____ My swimming class begins at nine thirty each morning.

_____ We change into our suits and quickly shower by nine thirty-five.

_____ If we're not sitting on the bench at the exact time, we will have five extra laps during our warm-up, which lasts for ten minutes.

_____ Then, we practice our strokes until five after ten.

_____ Next, we do rescue drills for ten minutes.

_____ Diving practice follows until ten twenty-five.

Punctuate these lists correctly.

1. There are several categories of swimmers beginner intermediate and advanced.

2. Many of my classmates are excellent divers namely Pete Carlos Susan Amanda and Yong.

3. Every day I take a bag of items to class swimsuit shampoo hairbrush and deodorant.

4. Today we practiced some strokes for example the breaststroke backstroke and butterfly.

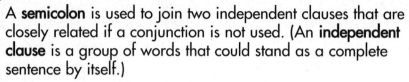

The History of the World

A **semicolon** is used to join two independent clauses that are closely related if a conjunction is not used. (An **independent clause** is a group of words that could stand as a complete sentence by itself.)

The Olympic Games originated in ancient Greece; the gods were important to the people of Greece. (Incorrect, these sentences are not closely related.)

The Olympic Games originated in ancient Greece; the main event was the pentathlon. (Correct, these sentences are closely related.)

Determine whether the following sentences are joined correctly. Write **Yes** on the line if they are; write **No** if they are not.

_____ 1. The Phoenicians were the most famous traders of the ancient world; they traded papyrus, ivory, glass, and wool.

_____ 2. The Persians built roads and canals; Alexander the Great's army defeated them.

_____ 3. Hittite rulers signed some of the first treaties; treaties helped to bring about peace.

_____ 4. Egyptian writing was based in hieroglyphics; the Egyptians worshiped many gods.

_____ 5. Ancient Greece was divided into city-states; Athens and Sparta were rivals.

_____ 6. Roman citizens were separated into two classes; the plebeians were commoners, and the patricians were nobles.

_____ 7. Charlemagne was a great ruler and warrior during medieval times; his kingdom extended over most of western Europe.

_____ 8. King John became king of England in 1199; he signed the Magna Carta.

Answer Key

Page 4
1. adjective
2. pronoun
3. conjunction
4. noun
5. preposition
6. article
7. verb
8. interjection
9. noun
10. adjective
11. verb
12. adverb

Page 5
while, and, not only, but also, so, either, or, yet, neither, nor, and, and, for

Page 6
1. can + not
2. are + not
3. do + not
4. does + not
5. is + not
6. has + not
7. must + not
8. have + not
9. will + not
10. had + not
11. should + not
12. need + not
13. could + not
14. were + not
15. did + not
16. might + not

1. I'm
2. he'll
3. it's
4. they'd
5. could've
6. I'd
7. we're
8. we'll

Page 7
1. G
2. J
3. A
4. F
5. B
6. H
7. C
8. D
9. E
10. I

1. J
2. E
3. H
4. I
5. A
6. F
7. B
8. G
9. C
10. D

Page 8
Help Wanted: -ing, -dom, -able, -ing, -ment
Meetings: -ance, -ing, -dom, -ship, -ness, -ment, -able

For Sale: -ade, -ing, -ing, -ness
Tutoring: -ing, -ure, -ing, -ful, -dom, -ful

Page 9
1. F
2. H
3. A
4. E
5. I
6. J
7. C
8. K
9. B
10. D
11. L
12. G

1. N
2. C
3. C
4. N
5. N
6. N
7. N
8. N

Page 10
Common Nouns: author, friends, family, clothes, money, school, book, stories, novel, books, life, readers, biography
Proper Nouns: Louisa May Alcott, Germantown, Pennsylvania, November, Ralph Waldo Emerson, Henry David Thoreau, Louisa, New England, Miss Alcott, *Flower Fables, Atlantic Monthly, Little Women, Little Men, Jo's Boys, Invincible Louisa*, Cornelia Meigs

Page 11
1. jackets
2. shirts
3. socks
4. dresses
5. sashes
6. swatches

1. boys
2. trays
3. sprays
4. treaties
5. ploys
6. mysteries

1. tomatoes
2. avocados
3. buffaloes
4. zoos
5. heroes
6. stereos

1. scarves
2. knives
3. leaves
4. chiefs
5. shelves
6. elves

Answer Key

Page 12

Concrete: Tony, cement, land, muscle, precipitation, sidewalk, New York, gravel, hardhat, road, shovel, truck, skyscraper, bucket, water, building, rock, mixer, trowel, street, asphalt, money, wood, glue, air, dog, book, man, music, sweat

Abstract: ambition, idea, trust, grace, hope, excitement, talent, honor, faith, sweetness, influence, zero, power, terror, beauty, argument, legacy, disgrace, victory, preference, love, fidelity, commitment, pride, hate, fear, integrity, evil, cooperation, improvement

Page 13

1. drummers' drumsticks
2. clarinet's reed
3. drum major's baton
4. musicians' instruments
5. tubas' sound
6. color guard's colorful flags
7. trombone's slide
8. cymbals' crash
9. band's new uniforms

Page 14

1. F	5. A	9. E
2. B	6. D	10. H
3. G	7. C	
4. J	8. I	

1. P; are	4. P; are
2. S; is	5. S; is
3. S; is	

Page 15

1. Reptiles = group
2. They = creatures
3. snake = reptile
4. swamp = home
5. Iguanas = members
6. They = lizards
7. desert = habitat
8. dinosaurs = reptiles
9. Tyrannosaurus = dinosaur

Page 16

1. O; it	5. S; He	9. S; We
2. S; It	6. S; I	10. O; me
3. O; us	7. O; him	11. O; him
4. S; I	8. O; her	12. O; it

Page 17

our = family
It = closet
their = everyone
it = pile
them = footwear
She = Maggie
They = boots, sandals, etc.
it = pile
it = mess
she = sister

Page 18

1. Everyone, loves
2. Several, play
3. some, practice
4. no one, knows
5. Many, choose, others, prefer
6. All, have
7. anyone, consider
8. Someone, claims
9. both, take
10. Each, races
11. somebody, was able

Page 19

Pronouns: him, her, her, them, his, his, we, he, his, him, our, him, his, Our, their, He, our, You('re), his, his, my, She, she, She, hers, It, me, mine, we, you

Possessive Pronouns: her, her, his, his, his, our, his, Our, their, our, his, his, my, hers, mine

Page 20

that, which, who, who, whose, that, which

1. I; Whose   5. I; Which
2. R; that   6. I; whom
3. R; who   7. R; which
4. R; which

Page 21
1. R; ourselves   7. R; yourself
2. I; itself   8. I; herself
3. I; himself   9. I; himself
4. I; myself   10. R; themselves
5. R; themselves   11. R; ourselves
6. R; herself   12. I; myself

Page 22
1. who   6. whom   11. who
2. whom   7. who   12. who
3. who   8. whom   13. who
4. who   9. who   14. whom
5. Who   10. who

Page 23
Action Verbs: presents, make, smile, fly, performing, dance, prance, bow, shoots, amaze, displays, flings
Being Verbs: are (experts), are (dressed), is (a sight), seem (royal), look (beautiful)

Page 24
1. occur, rises   6. blast
2. erupts, is   7. settles
3. contain   8. emerge, build
4. is destroyed   9. says
5. are

Page 25
1. P; comes   6. P; are grown
2. PA; treasured   7. P; have
3. PA; were called   8. F; will find
4. P; is called   9. P; are bitter
5. PA; drank   10. F; will be dried

Page 26
1. to create, to follow   6. to appear, to
2. To begin   move

3. to touch   7. to make
4. to form   8. to fold, to add
5. To continue   9. to design

Page 27
1. To cook
2. to shop for interesting ingredients
3. to visit her after school
4. to learn to make meatballs like Grandma's
5. To make spaghetti
6. to create chocolate-covered cream puffs

1. S; To give a great party
2. S; To write the guest list
3. PN; to plan the menu and decorations
4. PN; to celebrate with a Hawaiian theme
5. S; To offer her guests grass skirts and leis
6. S; To hula dance
7. S, To view her work
8. PN; to enjoy the party

Page 28
1. P; The entire class played the scavenger hunt game.
2. P; Mr. Mack, our homeroom teacher, divided the class into two teams.
3. A
4. A
5. P; Our teacher carefully hid all of the clues.

Page 29
thought, spent, drive, begun, ate, fallen, hide, wrote, written, speak, spoken, heard, heard, tear, tore, take, taken, wove, woven, steal, stolen, choose, chose

Page 30
1. pandas <u>seem</u> friendly and harmless
2. They <u>are</u> beautiful; They <u>look</u> teddy bears
3. panda <u>is</u> a native
4. people <u>are</u> extremely proud
5. Bamboo <u>is</u> food
6. forests <u>were</u> bountiful
7. biggest panda <u>was</u> almost 400 pounds;

Answer Key

average panda <u>weighs</u> over 200 pounds
8. cubs <u>can be</u> small
9. bones <u>are</u> large, thick, and very heavy
10. Pandas <u>seem</u> very happy

Page 31
1. PN; a mineralogist
2. PA; useful
3. PN; ore minerals
4. PA; uniquely beautiful
5. PA; green
6. PN; the diamond
7. PPN; it
8. PA; harder
9. PA; very soft
10. PPN; it
11. PN; specific gravity
12. PA; extremely heavy
13. PA; popular

Page 32
1. IT; Live bait
2. T; I, my new fishing hat
3. T; Dad, the tackle box
4. T; We, a sack lunch
5. T; I, fishing
6. IT; Dad
7. T; We, perch and catfish
8. IT; Our catch
9. T; I, baiting my own hook
10. T; I, a super big fish

Page 33
1. lays	5. laid	9. lie
2. lies	6. lying	10. lay
3. laid	7. laid	
4. lay	8. lay	

Page 34
1. set	5. sat	9. set
2. set	6. sit	10. set
3. sit	7. sat	11. set
4. set	8. sat	

Page 35
1. accept   2. affect   3. except   4. effect

1. accept   2. except   3. affects   4. effect

1. except   2. affect   3. effect   4. accept

Page 36
1. many slaves
2. none
3. freedom
4. none
5. the fugitives
6. any passengers
7. rewards
8. more than 750 slaves
9. her life

Page 37
1. was bringing, her grandmother
2. sold, the little pig
3. left, Baby Bear
4. to make, the shoemaker
5. gave, her
6. gave, her
7. handed, his mother
8. made, the emperor
9. gave, the wicked witch
10. gave, Sleeping Beauty
11. offered, the girl
12. told, the troll

Page 38
(For <u>some reason</u>), (of <u>America's most pop-ular hobbies</u>), (Aside from <u>ordinary stamp or coin collecting</u>), (of <u>all ages</u>), (from <u>unique pencil erasers</u>), (to <u>the ever-popular stuffed animals</u>), (for <u>many years</u>), (of <u>card</u>), (of <u>money</u>), (on <u>their collections</u>), (of <u>dol-lars</u>), (of <u>dollars</u>), (for <u>a single, yet desir-able, piece</u>), (for <u>their collection</u>), (Without <u>a doubt</u>), (over <u>many years</u>), (in <u>value</u>)

Page 39
1. about gods and goddesses—stories

Answer Key

2. from the Greek world—Myths
3. of the sea—god; of earthquakes and horses—god
4. of mythology—world; with many marvelous powers—gods, goddesses, and mortals
5. by Homer—the *Iliad* and the *Odyssey*
6. from ancient mythology—Eros; for love—quest
7. of the major Greek gods and goddesses—home
8. in the sky—Olympian
9. of love and beauty—goddess
10. in the underworld—home; of the dead—land
11. of music, poetry, and purity—god
12. for the gods—Messages

Page 40
1. in 1909, when
2. Since 1934, when
3. in the East Room, where
4. Inside the Green Room, where; on the floor, where
5. with green furnishings, how
6. by Martin Van Buren, how
7. in the Red Room, where
8. in the Yellow Oval Room, where
9. In 1941, when
10. In the Lincoln Bedroom, where

Page 41
Comparative: newer, more/less durable, cheaper, bigger, m/l comfortable, m/l beautiful, m/l creative, m/l proudly, m/l courageously, m/l quickly, m/l easily, m/l cheerfully, m/l safely, m/l slowly
Superlative: newest, most/least durable, cheapest, biggest, m/l comfortable, m/l beautiful, m/l creative, m/l proudly, m/l courageously, m/l quickly, m/l easily, m/l cheerfully, m/l safely, m/l slowly

Page 42
1. these	5. those	9. those
2. those	6. this	10. that
3. This	7. those	
4. these	8. these	

Page 43
1. this cotton candy
2. those bags of peanuts
3. these cups of soda
4. This pack of gummy pandas
5. that box of chocolates
6. those huge buckets of popcorn
7. that box of spiced candy
8. these candy bars

1. many, more
2. Each
3. Some
4. many
5. several
6. all

Page 44
1. was; cold and damp; cave
2. was; pitch dark; it
3. was; intimidating; litter of bats
4. were; wet; stalactites
5. were; shiny and beautiful; They
6. were; amazing; stalagmites
7. were; noisy; Droplets
8. were; unexplored; areas
9. was; informative; tour

Answers will vary.

Page 45
well, good, bad, well, good, badly, good, well, good, well, bad, badly, good

Page 46
sooner, soonest
harder, hardest
m/l noisily, m/l noisily
later, latest

Answer Key

m/l easily, m/l easily
m/l efficiently, m/l efficiently
m/l loudly, m/l loudly
m/l softly, m/l softly
m/l harshly, m/l harshly
m/l neatly, m/l neatly
m/l cheerfully, m/l cheerfully
m/l courageously, m/l courageously
m/l correctly, m/l correctly

Page 47

1. Negative Norman never seems to like anything.
2. On Saturday mornings when his mom makes him pancakes, he says, "I don't want any!"
3. When his buddies from school call, he will not talk to anyone.
4. Norman is so nasty he won't even feed his dog any food.
5. All day he just sits in his beanbag chair and won't ever go anywhere.
6. Norman doesn't seem to have any smile at all.
7. He obviously hasn't learned anything about enjoying life.

Page 48

1. Ancient; majestically in the golden desert sands of Egypt
2. The, Egyptian; nearly five thousand years ago
3. skilled, unskilled; together, to build the pyramids
4. Brilliant; carefully, thoughtfully
5. The, dangerous, difficult, of building pyramids; slowly and carefully
6. These incredibly large; especially for the pharoahs
7. Ancient; wholeheartedly
8. The, of dead kings; effectively, in the tombs

Page 49

1. After school; I have a key for getting into our locked house after school.
2. Under the flower pot; I always know I can find an extra key under the flower pot.
3. unfortunately; Unfortunately, the flower pot is missing.
4. In the basement; I consider breaking a window in the basement.
5. On the roof; I think about going down the chimney on the roof.
6. for an hour; Instead, I sit on the porch for an hour and wait for my mom to get home.

Page 50

Possible answers are:
1. Riding the big waves, they shouted excitedly from the water.
2. Lying in the sun, I was burned because my suntan lotion didn't work.
3. Playing barefoot, we had a volleyball game on the hot sand.
4. Tired and sandy, we ended our beach day.
5. Hanging out at the beach, we had a lot of fun.

Page 51

1. P	5. P	9. P
2. P	6. PA	10. PA
3. PA	7. P	11. PA
4. P	8. P	

Page 52

1. S; Cleaning
2. DO; cooking
3. OP; complaining
4. PN; procrastinating
5. S; Vacuuming
6. DO; dusting
7. DO; washing
8. S; Mopping
9. DO; making

Answer Key

10. S; Mowing the lawn
11. OP; pulling weeds
12. S; Washing dishes
13. PN; scrubbing the toilet

Page 53
1. During the Middle Ages,
2. At that time in European history,
3. In return for his loyalty,
4. Under the feudal system,
5. When a person controlled land,
6. At the age of about seven,
7. As soon as a squire had mastered the necessary skills,
8. As a knight,
9. Because they had few rights,
10. In return for clerical services,

Page 54
1. The teacher fell into the dunk tank when the baseball hit the target.
2. Her face turned bright red when she saw her undies being strung up the flagpole.
3. The pie hit her face when he threw it.
4. After he fell asleep, they sprayed shaving cream all over his head.
5. All the girls screamed after their canoe was tipped over.
6. He was so embarassed that he couldn't speak.
7. They put a worm on his plate while he was not looking.
8. Everyone laughed because she had a "kick-me" sign stuck to her back.

Independent Clause Underlined:
1. Jamie was sad because she didn't have enough money to go on the Ferris wheel.
2. After Jack ate two bags of cotton candy, he felt sick.
3. While Mrs. Brown wasn't looking, two kids snuck into the Tunnel O' Love.
4. The girls all cheered when the carnival strongman lifted two grown men over his head.

Page 55
1. DO; what they could do to earn money
2. DO; that his idea might work
3. S; What Felix proposed
4. S; That people would want their windows cleaned
5. S; How to get the proper equipment, PN; what they had to figure out first
6. S; whatever they could promise to persuade their customers
7. IO; whoever called in the first week
8. DO; that the fliers should be hand-delivered

Page 56
1. ADJ; that was like all the others
2. ADJ; that no one would forget
3. N; What Craig thought of
4. N; what we would do
5. ADV; because the snow packed so well
6. ADJ; who lives next door
7. N; What became the monster's body
8. ADV; after we hoisted the second ball on top of the first
9. ADV; To build his height

Page 57
1. PN; what make Christmas delicious
2. S; Whoever made this chocolate pie
3. DO; that this caramel corn isn't stale
4. IO; whoever says please
5. OP; whatever space she could find in her mouth

1. man who drives the ice-cream truck
2. honey that the bees make
3. jawbreaker, which was the size of a golf ball
4. bakery where my cousin works
5. fudge maker who worked in town

1. when; whenever you've eaten sweets
2. why; because he ate too much Halloween candy
3. when; At Christmastime

Answer Key

4. how; by dipping strawberries in melted chocolate

Page 58
1. or brain case
2. or collarbone
3. or scapulae
4. the sternum
5. the humerus; the radius and the ulna
6. or carpus
7. finger and toe bones
8. his kneecap
9. the large tibia and the slender fibula
10. the femur

Page 59
Simple Subject Underlined:
<u>trees</u>, tempted, <u>we</u>, could smell, <u>apples</u>, decorated, <u>We</u>, strained, <u>thought</u>, made, <u>Mrs. Haggly</u>, was, <u>Everyone</u>, knew, <u>She</u>, had, <u>She</u>, bent, <u>people</u>, thought, <u>we</u>, decided, was, <u>that</u>, <u>brother</u>, ran, <u>I</u>, followed, <u>we</u>, had, <u>we</u>, went, <u>we</u>, ate, <u>They</u>, were, <u>we</u>, paid, did, <u>we</u>, ache, <u>stomachs</u>, grew, <u>We</u>, were, <u>story</u>, has, <u>apples</u>, are, <u>ladies</u>, are

Page 60
1. CS; my sister and I
2. CP; pick the apples and wash them well
3. CS; Tami and I
4. CP; will be too chunky and will not work
5. CP; eats an apple or sneaks some caramels
6. CP; starts dipping and turning the first apple in the hot caramel
7. CS; Mom and Dad
8. CP; roll a few apples in the nuts and leave some plain
9. CP; will devour and enjoy them for dessert
10. CP; love to make caramel apples but hate to clean up the sticky mess and put away all the dishes

Page 61
Punctuation may vary slightly.
1. D; .
2. IN; ?
3. IM; .
4. D; .
5. IN; ?
6. D; .
7. D; .
8. IM; .
9. E; ! or IN; ?
10. D; .
11. IN; ?

Page 62
1. S
2. C
3. S
4. S
5. S
6. C
7. C
8. S
9. C
10. S

Page 63
1. which is a cousin to the moth
2. whose bodies are partly covered with multicolored scales
3. Because of its many rows of scales
4. which is made up of thousands of tiny lenses
5. which are located on the top of its head
6. Because the butterfly is often in search of nectar
7. While it searches for nectar
8. which helps the flowers reproduce

Page 64
Independent Clauses Underlined:
1. Because the weather is turning cold, <u>I will go south, and I will join others like myself</u>.
2. <u>I can weigh more than ten elephants</u>, and when I am fully grown, <u>my length is greater than a four-story building</u>.
3. <u>Scientists</u>, who are called cetologists, <u>know we have black and white markings, but our markings differ from one another</u>.
4. Though we all have similar markings, <u>our individual ones are just as unique as a person's fingerprints, and they are as individual as a giraffe's spots</u>.
5. <u>I have a big tail, and I like to flip it up</u>

Answer Key

when I am traveling.
6. My skin, which covers my entire body, is smooth and hairless, but it is bumpy on parts of my head.
7. Although I eat huge amounts of food, I have no teeth, instead I have baleens.
8. If I rise out of the water, you might see my dorsal fins, or I might show you a glimpse of my tail.
9. Underneath my skin is a thick layer of dense fatty tissue, which is called blubber, and it maintains my body temperature at 93° to 99° F (34° to 37° C).

Page 65
1. C
2. S
3. CX
4. S
5. C-CX
6. CX
7. S
8. C-CX
9. S
10. C

Page 66
1. E
2. D
3. B
4. OK
5. A
6. H
7. OK
8. C
9. OK
10. F
11. G

Page 67
Answers may vary slightly.
1. rocks. He
2. OK
3. head, but they
4. arms, and they
5. position. The male
6. scavengers. Most are
7. echinoderms. Their bodies
8. OK

Page 68
1. d; elephant-like
2. a; dur-ing
3. a; mam-moths
4. b; twenty-five
5. a; use-ful
6. d; three-horned
7. d; razor-sharp
8. c; one-half
9. b; forty-seven

Page 69
1. DQ; Jennifer asked, "Did you see Rae's hair? It is bright orange!"
2. DQ; "She dyed it herself," said Jordan.
3. DQ; "Yeah," Tamara said with a sneer, "she needs a wig."

1. DQ; "I'll see you at the party," declared Paige.
2. DQ; "What party?" asked Maya.
3. DQ; "Steve's brothers are giving him a surprise birthday party," answered Paige, "and everyone is going."
4. IQ

1. DQ; "Don't look now," warned Jeff, "but Robby is about to drink his pop."
2. DQ; "So what?" Anna asked.
3. IQ
4. IQ

Page 70
9:30, 9:35, 9:45, 10:05, 10:15, 10:25

1. There are several categories of swimmers: beginner, intermediate, and advanced.
2. Many of my classmates are excellent divers, namely, Pete, Carlos, Susan, Amanda, and Yong.
3. Every day I take a bag of items to class: swimsuit, shampoo, hairbrush, and deodorant.
4. Today we practiced some strokes, for example, the breaststroke, backstroke, and butterfly.

Page 71
1. Y
2. N
3. Y
4. N
5. Y
6. Y
7. Y
8. N